D1631909

THE
SCOTTISH
HEATHER
BOOK

Brian D. Osborne

Illustrated by Gerard Bradley

Appletree Press

First published by The Appletree Press Ltd
19-21 Alfred Street, Belfast BT2 8DL
Tel: +44 (0) 1232 243074
Fax: +44 (0) 1232 246756
E-mail: frontdesk@appletree.ie
Website: www.irelandseye.com

The Scottish Heather Book

ISBN 0-86281-705-6

CONTENTS

"The bonnie bloomin' heather"

Scotland enjoys a rich variety of emblematic plants associated with the nation. Hugh MacDiarmid's "little white rose of Scotland" has its honoured place as has the majestic Scots pine (Pinus sylvestris), *the characteristic tree of the old, and now all but vanished, Caledonian forest. However, two plants surely must, above all others, take their place as recognised symbols of Scotland and Scottishness – the thistle and the heather. Let James Hogg, "The Ettrick Shepherd", carry forward our argument:*

"What are the flowers of Scotland,
All others that excel,
The lovely flowers of Scotland,
All others that excel?
The thistle's purple bonnet,
And bonny heather-bell,
Oh, they're the flowers of Scotland,
All others that excel!"

The thistle has found itself a significant place in national heraldry and symbolism, and its "wha daur meddle wi' me" prickliness most certainly reflects a distinct element in the Scottish character. However, heather has, in its own quieter way, become a much used and much loved symbol of the nation. Postcards, shortbread tins and whisky bottles all alike testify to the representational quality of this plant. Quite why this is so will, hopefully, emerge more fully from the rest of this book but undoubtedly there is something in the idea of the hardy heather plant flourishing in a harsh upland environment which speaks to the self-image of the Scot. Be that as it may, heather has certainly aroused the deep emotions of Scots (and visitors to Scotland), inspired poetry and song, played a significant part in the economy of the country, sheltered her people and been widely used as a symbol of nationhood and a badge of identity. While there is no species of heather unique to Scotland, it (or rather they, for as we shall discover we have three species) has nonetheless become a shorthand expression of Scottishness. Heather has, in short, found its way into a great many unexpected corners of Scotland and Scottish life and this book seeks to record and celebrate both the familiar and some of the less expected connections between Scotland and the "bonnie bloomin' heather".

The word "heather" itself is of interest, although more than a little confusing. Earlier spellings include: *hathir, haddyr, haddir, heddir* and all may perhaps be derived from the same root as "heath"; that is from a word found in a variety of Germanic languages and meaning "open uncultivated land". *The Oxford English Dictionary* notes that heather in the familiar modern spelling first appears in the eighteenth century as a Scottish form of "heath", and although the *Scottish National Dictionary* records the modern spelling as early as 1584 earlier forms, as we shall discover, survived into the eighteenth century. There is, however, some doubt about the connection between "heath" and "heather" and the *Oxford English Dictionary* suggests that the older Scottish forms such as "hedder" could be expected to have other origins and that the association between the Southern English "heath" and the Scottish "hedder" is comparatively recent. Such

etymological disputes aside, "heath" is used in English both as a word to describe open moorland and for one of a variety of ericaceous plants, while Scottish usage normally reserves the word "heath" for the location and "heather" for the plant. However poets, even Scots ones, being poets, frequently use heath for the plant (it is after all a syllable shorter and this can at times be useful!).

Whatever may be one's state of knowledge or confusion about the varieties of the plant, or the origins of the name, the one certain fact about heather which everyone knows is that white heather is lucky. Queen Victoria, visiting Dunrobin in Sutherland, records in her diary the activity of her faithful Highland servant John Brown:

hn Brown and Queen Victoria

"Brown (who has an extraordinary eye for it, when driving quite fast, which I have not) espied a piece of white heather and jumped off to pick it. No Highlander would pass it by without picking it, for it is considered to bring good luck."

Calluna vulgaris

Quite why white heather is thought to be lucky is obscure. White heather does not form a separate species and is simply a more or less uncommon variant of the normal pink or purple flowered plant. All three of our native species are to be found in white forms although the commonest is the white variant of *Calluna vulgaris*, the common heather or ling. The comparative rarity of the white form presumably accounts for the belief in the luck-bringing property of white heather.

The popularity of white heather is said to have been enhanced in the nineteenth century when the future Kaiser Frederick of Germany presented Princess Victoria, the Princess Royal, with a bunch of white heather when he proposed to her. One further indication of the popularity of heather has been its increasing adoption, since the nineteenth century, as a girl's name. In Scotland it is within the Top 50 most popular names.

With its wide spread throughout the Highlands it is not surprising that the people of the Highlands adopted heather as a symbol and a clan badge. A seventeenth century manuscript describes the appearance of a Highland military force:

"... among the ensigns, besides other singularities, the Glencow men were verie remarkable, who had for their ensign a faire bush of heather, well spread and displayed on the head of a staff."

The "Glencow men" would be the Macdonalds of

Clan emblem, Macdonalds of Glencoe

Glencoe, whose badge, along with the other branches of this widespread clan, was the common heather or ling, *Calluna vulgaris*. In the Gaelic, which would have been spoken by the Macdonalds, the common heather or ling is known as *fraoch*. The clan still has the same badge. However, a sprig in the cap-badge is now a more normal way of showing the clan affiliation than the "fair bush... well spread and displayed". The bell heather *(Erica cinerea)*, in Gaelic *fraoch a'bhadain* – the tufted heather – was used as the badge of Clan Robertson or Donnachaidh. No clan seems to have claimed the cross-leaved heather *(Erica tetralix)*, in Gaelic *fraoch Frangach* – French heather, for a badge, nor, doubtless due to its scarcity, has the white form of ling *(fraoch geal* in the Gaelic) been adopted for this purpose.

So, metaphorically clutching our lucky white heather, let us explore, in the company of poets, novelists, travellers, and a host of others, the history and associations of this, perhaps the most loved of all Scotland's plants.

"A sprig of white heather I pluck'd on the brae"

Heather is the characteristic and predominant plant of much of the Scottish moorland and to most people heather is just heather. However, as we have seen, Scotland has three native species of heather.

Much the commonest of the three is the plant frequently called ling, Scotch heather, or just simply "heather" and which is scientifically known as *Calluna vulgaris*. It has bright pink flowers borne on a dense growth of spikes. The construction of the flowers is different from the other heathers in that the calyx almost conceals the petals, while in the other species the petals cover the calyx. It was this distinction, first noted by Richard Salisbury in 1801 in a paper to the Linnaean Society, which resulted in the removal of this plant from the Erica family and its placing in its own genus.

Erica tetralix

are carried at the end of the branches. Our third native species is the cross-leaved heath or bog heather *(Erica tetralix)*. This latter plant is somewhat less common than the others and tends to flourish in moister areas and has pale pink flowers and greyish leaves which cross over each other hence one of its common names. Its scientific name is in fact also derived from its characteristic leaf arrangement of four leaves in a whorl, as opposed to the three leaves in a whorl arrangement of *Erica cinerea*. Both these species reach a maximum height of 60 centimetres. All three species occur in white-flowered forms.

Calluna vulgaris is the tallest growing of our three species – reaching one metre in favourable conditions. It is most frequently found in the drier eastern side of the country.

The other heathers widely found are bell heather *(Erica cinerea)* – a smaller shrub than the common heather and typically found in drier sites, its purple red flowers

Although the three species described above are those which are widely distributed in Scotland and in suitable areas of England there are also a number of locally occuring heaths found in south-west England. These include the Dorset heath *(Erica ciliaris)*, Cornish Heath *(Erica vagans)*; while species found in Ireland include the Irish heath *(Erica mediterranea)* and *Erica mackaiana*. There are also a number of related species of ericaceous plants such as blaeberry, cowberry, bearberry which are to be found in similar moorland environments to the heathers.

The three Scottish heathers are typically found in acid peat moorlands. Peat results from the slow and incomplete breaking down of vegetable matter in cold and wet conditions. The heathers manage to survive in these poor, nitrogen deficient, soils because of their ability to utilise fungal parasites in their roots to fix atmospheric nitrogen.

The various Scottish species of heather mainly occur between 150 and 450 metres above sea level, although specimens can be found from sea level to around the 750 metre level. Despite their origins in hostile conditions in these high peat moors, heathers have become popular garden plants.

Three species of Scottish heather

Muirburn

A wide range of cultivated varieties have been developed by nurseries from both the *Calluna* and *Erica* species as well as from foreign species. Such is the skill of the cultivator that this group of plants can provide flower and foliage colour the year round. Heather nurseries have sprung up in many areas of Scotland to cater for this high demand. The ease of maintenance and ground covering characteristics of the heaths and heathers have resulted in widespread park and garden planting in areas with suitable, non-alkaline soils. However, even the presence of alkaline soil need not totally preclude the enjoyment of heathers as some of the foreign species such as Corsican heath and *Eric carnea* are tolerant of limy or chalky conditions.

Heather has a complex life cycle, extending over a period of around 40 or 50 years, with distinct phases of growth, development, maturity and decay. As a forage plant for game birds, sheep and deer, heather needs to be managed to maintain young healthy growth to maximise its food value. This management is usually carried out by the process known in Scotland as muirburn. Areas of mature heather are set alight,

hopefully under carefully controlled conditions, promoting colonisation and re-growth of young heather. The procedure thus artificially keeps large parts of the heather moors at a highly productive stage just before maturity. In order to provide cover for the birds some stands of mature heather are best left and thus the burning is carried out in small sections, giving a varied, patchwork effect. In areas of better growth this burning may be done every ten years or so. In wetter areas, with slower growth and less dense coverage, the burning needs to be done less frequently.

Muirburn has long been controlled both by law and by tenancy agreements. The Scottish Parliament, in 1424 and 1535, introduced legislation to regulate the practice and in 1773 the UK

Parliament enacted "An Act for the more effectual preservation of game in that part of Great Britain called Scotland", which set the time limits for muirburn as 1 November to 11 April with a possible extension to 25 April for owners of high and wet moorlands.

Such legal and official interest in the process of muirburn reflects the significance of heather in the diet of both game birds, deer and sheep. In particular the red grouse *(Lagopus scoticus)* is, for a large part of the year, dependent on heather shoots, flowers and seeds for much of its diet. Other mountain dwelling species of game birds, such as ptarmigan and black grouse also browse on heather. Both grouse and heather thrive best on the drier hills of the east of Scotland and large areas of these hills are carefully managed for sporting interests and sheep-grazing. The "natural" or "wilderness" appearance of a Cairngorm hillside covered in a thick growth of heather is thus an entirely artificial, man-made result; a product of the clearance of the ancient native forest and of generations of management by grazing and controlled burning.

Red and black grouse

"Ane herbe... richt nutritive baith to beistis and fowlis"

The visitor, admiring a hillside in the Cairngorms, glorious in its late summer purple, seldom gives much thought to the wider economic role of heather. Sufficient that it should feed the grouse, look romantic and assist the profits of Kodak or Agfa.

Heather, however, is a plant of some economic importance, quite apart from its role as fodder for grouse. Our ancestors thought highly of the plant. In the words of the sixteenth-century historian Hector Boece:

"... in all the desertis and muris of this realme growis ane herbe, namit hadder... richt nutritive baith to beistis and fowlis; specialie to beis. This herbe, in the moneth of July, hes ane floure of purpure hew, als sweit as huny."

Picts brewing heather ale

This "richt nutritive" plant was employed for a variety of useful purposes, even being turned into a range of drinks.

The most mysterious and romantic of these drinks – heather ale – was apparently made by a secret recipe now supposed to be lost. Legend tells how a Pictish father and son, the last custodians of the mystery, were being tortured to make them reveal the method. In some versions the torturer was Kenneth MacAlpin, who died in 858 and was the first ruler over both the Scots and the Picts; in others the Vikings were the guilty party. In either case the object was to secure the secret of this delectable drink made from the tops and blossoms of the plant. The father, fearing his son's fortitude and wishing to spare him further suffering,

agreed to reveal the secret providing his son was first swiftly killed. This being done he defied his captors to do their worst to him and the secret of heather ale died with him. Boece in *The Bounds of Albion* generalises the story and notes that:

"The Pichtis maid of this herbe, sum time, ane richt delicius and hailsum drink. Nochtheless, the manner of the making of it is perist, be exterminioun of the said Pichtis out of Scotland; for they schew nevir the craft of the making of this drink bot their awin blud."

Robert Louis Stevenson retells the story in his poem *Heather Ale: A Galloway Legend,* which starts:

"From the bonny bells of heather
They brewed a drink longsyne

Was sweeter far than honey,
Was stronger far than wine.
They brewed it and they drank it,
And lay in a blessed swound
For days and days together
In their dwellings underground."

The poet and novelist Neil Munro gives yet another version in his short story *The Secret of the Heather-Ale*, setting the action around his native Inveraray. James Logan in *The Scottish Gael* claims that a relic of the production of heather ale may be seen in the many areas of Highland moorland which are level and stone free:

"... they are believed to have been the fields cleared by the Picts for the cultivation of the heath, which they mowed down when in bloom".

In the *Second Statistical Account of the Wigtownshire Parish of Kirkmaiden*, the parish minister, the Rev John Lamb, writing in the 1840s, refers to:

"... two small green eminences, called the 'Auld Kilns', situated among surrounding heath. These, tradition says, were used by Picts in preparing their mysterious beverage..."

The mystery of heather ale is compounded, and fears arise that the deaths of so many last possessors of the secret may have been in vain, because the well-known twentieth-century authority on Scottish food F. Marion MacNeill provides a recipe for it in her books *The Scots Kitchen* and *The Scots Cellar*. This recipe involves some fairly ordinary processes and nothing more mysterious than heather, hops, yeast, sugar, ginger and water. One might, of course, question the Picts' access to ginger and hops and however refreshing this brew may be it hardly seems likely to live up to the magical reputation passed on to us by the poets and story-tellers. It may well indeed be the case that some vanished process or ingredient gave the Pictish original its potency, both imaginative and alcoholic.

Logan also recalls that old-time Highland home-brewers invariably put the green tops of heather in to the mash tub to add to the strength and flavour of their beer. Confirmation comes from the eighteenth-century traveller Thomas Pennant who mentions that, in the island of Islay, ale was made from:

"... the tops of young heath, mixed with a third part of malt and a few hops."

Scottish wildcat and field mouse

It seems that in some places the roots were also used, but with caution due to their astringent qualities.

In 1993, a Glasgow company, Glenbrew, started to produce a modern heather ale – *Leann Fraoch* – from a small brewery in Taynuilt. This brew, based on a traditional Hebridean recipe, used heather flowers to give it aroma and astringency. So successful was the new ale that production transferred

Erica cinera

to the larger Thistle Brewery in Alloa. *Leann Fraoch* is now widely available in draught and bottled form.

In his famous description of the whisky industry, *Whisky Distilleries of the United Kingdom*, first published in 1887, the author Alfred Barnard, visiting Highland Park Distillery in Orkney, is taken to their "Heather House".

"Here heather is stored, which has been gathered in the month of July, when the blossom is fully set. It is carefully cut off near the root, and tied into small faggots of about a dozen branches. One or two of these faggots are used with the peat in drying the malt every time the fire is made up, and imparts a delicate flavour of its own to the malt, rendering Highland

Park Whisky unlike any other made in the kingdom. To convince us of this, a few sprigs, well covered with dried blossoms, were thrown into an open chauffeur with a small quantity of peat, and we must confess that we detected a most pronounced odour, and quite different from the peat when used alone."

Sadly, this practice has been abandoned, and bundles of flowering heather no longer flavour this splendid Orcadian malt whisky. Highland Park's Manager, James Robertson, confirms that:

"... Heather is not used in our kilns and... it has not been used in the memory of this or the previous generation of maltmen. I must assume therefore that it ceased in the early 1900s."

However, at least one guide to malt whiskies, relying perhaps over much on Barnard's classic text, and on tradition and imagination, reports confidently that heather is still used and can indeed be tasted in the finished dram. To be fair, the peat used will contain decomposed heather but the distinctive effect Barnard describes clearly relied on the use of fresh heather as an additive.

Where heather can without doubt be tasted is in heather honey – the blossoms of heather producing a fine nectar attractive to both wild and domesticated bees. While heather honey is still a popular delicacy, widely available, the honey from wild bees is now a rarity, a great decline in the wild bee population seemingly having occured in the nineteenth

Boys collecting heather honey

century. Osgood MacKenzie, the creator of Inverewe Gardens in Wester Ross, writing in his classic volume of memoirs, *A Hundred Years in the Highlands*, records:

"I often heard, when I was young, that in the Lews (whose poetical name in Gaelic is *Eilan an Fhraoich*, the Heather Island) bees were so plentiful in the olden times that the boys were able to collect large quantities of wild honey, which, by applying heat to it, was run into glass bottles and sold at the Stornoway markets. Hunting for wild bees' nests was one of the great ploys for the boys in the autumn, but nowadays this amusement is never thought of."

Heather honey is, of course, an essential ingredient in the well-known delicacy of *Athole Brose* – a mixture of heather honey, whisky and oatmeal.

The good things of heather were not reserved solely for man; in the hill country of Strathdon in Aberdeenshire heather was formerly cut in the summer and dried as winter forage for farm animals. In the Lammermuir hills of the eastern Borders the herds in the last century distinguished between the superior type of fodder provided by *Calluna vulgaris* or ling and the inferior fodder represented by *Erica cinerea* – the bell heather.

The all-providing heather furnished our forebears with a comfortable bed, although the intrepid Sarah Murray in her pioneering travel guide, *A Companion and Useful Guide to the Beauties of Scotland*, first published in 1799, thought little of such accommodation.

27

She remarked of some dwellings which she visited near Fort William:

"... I hardly saw any difference between the huts and the moor; for what heath there was on either was equally in bloom. At night they rake out the fire, and put their beds of heath and blankets... on the ground, where the fire had been, and thus keep themselves warm during the night... A person accustomed to the comforts and luxuries of life cannot conceive how it is possible for human beings to exist in a state so near to that of brute creation."

The great sixteenth-century historian and classical scholar George Buchanan, in his *Description of Scotland* (1582), gives a more enthusiastic description of the merits of a heather bed as used by the Highlanders.

His Latin original was translated by Thomas Aikman in 1821:

"In their houses, also, they lie upon the ground; strewing fern or heath on the floor, with the roots downward and the leaves turned up. In this manner they form a bed so pleasant that it may vie in softness with the finest down, while in salubrity it far exceeds it, for heath, naturally possessing the power of absorption, drinks up the superfluous moisture, and restores strength to the fatigued nerves, so that those who lie down languid and weary in the evening, arise in the morning, vigorous and sprightly."

An equally enthusiastic view of the heather bed was given by the eighteenth-century Scottish novelist Tobias Smollett in his comic

Highlanders on heather beds

masterpiece *The Expedition of Humphry Tinker*. Jerry Melfort writes from Argyleshire to say that:

"... My Uncle and I were indulged with separate chambers and down beds, which we begged to exchange for a layer of heath, and indeed I never slept so much to my satisfaction. It was not only soft and elastic, but the plant, being in flower, diffused an agreeable fragrance, which is wonderfully refreshing and restorative."

Heather also provided shelter from the elements for the Highlander. In favourable conditions *Calluna vulgaris* will grow to a metre in height and can be used for thatching roofs or for combining with mud and grass into a type of daub and wattle construction. While buildings formed in such a way could not be expected to survive long in the wet conditions of the Highlands, the use of heather thatch was widespread and eminently practical despite the comments of the English traveller Thomas Pennant who, on his Scottish tour in 1769, noted of Glen Tilt in Perthshire that:

"... the houses of the common people in these parts are shocking to humanity, formed of loose stones, and covered with clods, which they call devols, or with heath, broom, or branches of fir; they look, at a distance, like so many black mole-hills."

However, a heather-thatched roof had one obvious disadvantage, it was highly flammable. In the early

ammable heather roof

sixteenth century a feud broke out between the Drummonds and the Murrays. During this dispute the Murrays retreated and sheltered in a church, the Drummonds respected this sanctuary and withdrew; as they did so however they were fired on by the Murrays from the shelter of the church. Enraged by this treacherous behaviour the Drummonds set alight the heather roof of the church and burned the unfortunate Murrays to death.

In a more technological and peaceable age, heather still

had its part to play in construction work. When in the 1890s the West Highland Railway was being constructed between Glasgow and Fort William the engineers experienced great difficulty in constructing the line across the bogs of the great Rannoch Moor. They were forced to use bundles of heather and brushwood as the first foundation for the soil, rock and ash infill. The modern railway track thus, in effect, floats on a bed of heather – truly a versatile and valuable plant.

Heather was traditionally used for brush making and heather brooms or besoms may still be purchased for garden use. The extent to which heather was used for such domestic purposes may be judged by the survival of an old Edinburgh street cry:

"Fine heather reenges, better never grew;
Fine heather reenges, wha'll buy them noo?
Besoms for a penny, reenges for a plack;
If ye winna buy them, help them on my back."

A reenge or range was a pot scourer made from bundles of heather. These it seems from the rhyme cost a plack- or four pennies Scots, that is one-third of the penny sterling: the price being asked by the packman for a besom or broom. The finer and more pliable and less scratchy cross-leaved heath, *Erica tetralix*, was normally used for making reenges. In fact an alternative Gaelic name for *Erica tetralix* was *Fraoch an ruinnse*, the rinsing heath, from just this use. The longer, tougher stems of *Calluna vulgaris* were employed in broom making.

Glen Douglas on Rannoch Moor, 1912

Edinburgh, 1775

It is, indeed, this use as a broom which gave heather or ling its scientific name *Calluna*, the word being derived from the Greek *Kalluna* – to adorn or to sweep.

The old herbals recommended the use of heather for a variety of medical problems:

"The tender tops and flowers are goode to be laide upon the bitings or stingings of any venomous beast"

while Dodoens's *Historie of Plants* speaks of the benefits of a:

"... decoction of our common heath made with faire water to be drunken warm both morning and evening, in the quantity of five ounces, three hours before meat, against the stone in the bladder."

Neither of these remedies are recommended to readers.

Food, medicine, building material, bedding, and pot-scourer – there seems to be no end to the versatility of the heather – it could of course also be used for fuel. In his *History of Greater Britain*, published in 1521, John Major recorded that:

"Heather or bog-myrtle grows in the moors in greatest abundance, and for fuel is but little less serviceable than juniper... Some of our countrymen suppose the land on which this plant is found to be worthless and barren; but I, on the other hand, look upon it as eminently valuable and fruitful ground. The plant when dried after the manner of juniper makes excellent fuel, and I much prefer it to coal..."

Almost 300 years later, Dorothy Wordsworth, on her tour of Scotland in 1803, paid a visit to a "Highland hut" in Glengyle and was given a hospitable Highland welcome by the woman of the house who:

"heaped up some dry peats and heather, and, blowing it with her breath, in a short time raised a blaze that scorched us with comfortable feelings."

Throughout the Highlands and other upland areas, the stalks and roots of burned heather or "heather-birns" were widely used as kindling and fuel. John Buchan, incidentally, uses the image of dried up and wizened heather birns to describe the witch Alison Sempill in his supernatural story *The Outgoing of the Tide*:

"... there in the corner sat the weird-wife Alison, dead as a stone and shrivelled like a heather birn."

"Ca' the ewes to the knowes
Ca' them whare the heather grows"

Heather, perhaps surprisingly, had quite a bad press in early literature. Shakespeare rather set the tone with his reference in Macbeth to "a blasted heath" and even the storm-tossed Gonzalo in The Tempest *only cries: "Now I would give a thousand furlongs of sea for an acre of barren ground — long heath, brown furze, anything" in his understandable anxiety to avoid a watery grave.*

It must be remembered that until the taste for the romantic and the picturesque developed at the end of the eighteenth century the wild and uncultivated nature of the heather clad Scottish mountain sides struck most travellers as, in Dr Johnson's words, "a wide extent of hopeless sterility".

Boswell and Johnson travelled widely through the Highlands and Islands, including some of the prime heather growing areas of the eastern Highlands, and that at a season when the heather was in flower. However, the Doctor's only observation is the somewhat grudging remark that the hills were:

"... almost wholly covered with dark heath, and even that seems to be checked in its growth."

while Boswell has no comment to offer on the subject at all.

The great agricultural improver Sir John Sinclair, the creator of the Old and New Statistical Accounts, well expressed the pre-romantic view of heather in his *Analysis of the Statistical Account of Scotland* published in 1825:

"The mountains, in some parts of the Highlands, were, a few years ago, covered with heath; but many of them, by being pastured with sheep, are now rendered almost entirely green, and, from the rapidity with which this change has taken place, it is likely that the heath will soon be very generally extirpated, and the value of the ground by that means considerably improved."

Even that enthusiastic admirer of Scotland's scenery the Court of Session judge Lord Cockburn had a somewhat utilitarian attitude to heather. In 1841 he wrote in his *Circuit Journeys* of visiting Kindrogan in Perthshire where:

"Sheep and turf are encroaching on heather and muirfowl. There is no better

Black-faced sheep in heather

pasture on any Highland hills."

However, 12 years later he confided to his diary:

"I think it my duty to record the unmatched merits of a leg of mutton we had at dinner today. It was a leg which stands out even amidst the legs of my long and steadily muttonised life... It spoke of winter straths and summer heights, of tender heather, Alpine airs, cold springs, and that short sweet grass which corries alone can cherish..."

Even a poet and novelist like James Hogg, "The Ettrick Shepherd", travelling through the Highlands in the early summer of 1803 could note critically in a letter to Walter Scott that:

"The braes of Glenorchy have no very promising

appearance, being much over-run with heath..."

However, as we will see when he was in poetic mode, Hogg's view of the national plant was somewhat more positive.

Visiting Scotland just a few months after Hogg's tour were William and Dorothy Wordsworth and their friend, Samuel Coleridge. At Boniton Linn, Dorothy noted a habit that has endured to the present day. Writing of a party of English tourists, she observed, with all the disdain of a traveller for a tourist:

"... they had stuffed the pockets of their carriage with bundles of heather, roots and all, just as if Scotland grew no heather but on the banks of the Clyde."

The Wordsworths were of course visiting Scotland in

the late summer and early autumn – the peak time of heather blossom. Near Loch Katrine, Dorothy was moved to note that:

"The heather was indeed the most luxuriant I ever saw; it was so tall that a child of ten years old struggling through it would often have been buried head and shoulders, and the exquisite beauty of the colour, near or at a distance, seen under the trees, is not to be conceived."

An enthusiasm for the plant echoed by a later visitor to the same area; the noted heather-lover Queen Victoria, whose diary of a visit to the Trossachs in September 1869 gives the following enthusiastic descriptions of heather and hill near Aberfoyle:

"... here the splendid scenery begins – high, rugged, and green hills... very fine large

Blaeberries

trees and beautiful pink heather, interspersed with bracken, rocks, and underwood, in the most lovely profusion, and Ben Lomond towering up before us with its noble range."

Near Loch Ard, the Queen observed:

"The heather is in full bloom, and of the richest kind, some almost of a crimson colour, and growing in rich tufts along the road."

Her Majesty concluded that:

"This solitude, the romance and wild loveliness of everything here... the independent simple people, who all speak Gaelic here, all make beloved Scotland the proudest, finest country in the world. Then there is that beautiful heather, which you do not see elsewhere. I prefer it greatly to Switzerland, magnificent and glorious as the scenery of that country is."

Novelists have, of course, made good use of heather as a setting for their action. A large part of Robert Louis Stevenson's *Kidnapped* is devoted to the moorland

adventures of David Balfour and Alan Breck Stewart. Indeed, three chapters have as their title "The Flight in the Heather". The two heroes sleep on beds of heather and escape from the pursuing redcoats across the wastes of Rannoch Moor:

"Much of it was red with heather."

However, David and Alan also have to cross a stretch which had been burned:

"All the time, too, he kept winding in and out in the lower parts of the moorland where we were best concealed. Some of these had been burned or at least scathed with fire; and there rose in our faces (which were close to the ground) a blinding, choking dust as fine as smoke."

Equally memorable for a flight across a heather moor

David Balfour and Alan Breck Stewart

is Richard Hannay's escape from the Black Stone gang in John Buchan's *The Thirty-Nine Steps*. Hannay faced a different sort of search, his enemies were equipped with aircraft and he quickly realises that:

"These heather hills were no sort of cover if my enemies were in the sky..."

Wisely he leaves the Galloway uplands for the shelter of the wooded valleys.

The idea of heather as a hiding place is of course older than Buchan or Stevenson and "to take to the heather" has, in literature and in life, become a commonplace expression for escaping from the law. An idea which perhaps owes something to the Covenanters and their moorland conventicles. Another familiar heather-related expression, "to set the heather on fire", means to create a sensation or a disturbance and Walter Scott uses it in this sense in *Rob Roy* when Rob Roy MacGregor remarks to Francis Osbaldistone about one of the complexities of his romance with Diana Vernon:

"And it's partly that whilk has set the heather on fire e'en now."

Economists, agriculturalists, diarists and novelists may all, in their different ways, have had something of interest and relevance to say about heather, but it is surely the poets who have most memorably celebrated the heather. Even James Hogg, who we noted earlier casting a shepherd's baleful eye at the lack of good grazing on the braes of Glenorchy, used heather as a setting for many a poem, for example in *The Skylark*:

"Then, when the gloaming comes,
Low in the heather blooms
Sweet will thy welcome and bed of love be!
Emblem of happiness
Blest is thy dwelling-place
O, to abide in the desert with thee!"

In more stirring and patriotic mode, the heather is the setting for his Jacobite *McLean's Welcome*:

"Come o'er the stream, Charlie,
Dear Charlie, brave Charlie,
Come o'er the stream, Charlie,
And dine with McLean,
If aught will invite you,
Or more will delight you,
'Tis ready, a troop of our bold Highlandmen,

All ranged on the heather,
With bonnet and feather,
Strong arms and broad claymores,
Three hundred and ten."

Robert Burns, who of course shared an agricultural background with Hogg, frequently used heather as setting for his verse from the early poem *Song*, composed in August, a work of his teenage years, he writes:

"Now westlin winds, and slaught'ring guns
Bring autumn's pleasant weather;
The moorcock springs, on whirring wings
Amang the blooming heather."

Later in one of the last songs, he contributed to the Scots Musical Museum:

"As I cam o'er the Cairney mount,

And down amang the blooming heather,
Kindly stood the milkin-shiel
To shelter frae the stormy weather".

Both verses perhaps suffer from the rather cliched image of the " blooming heather" and the over-easy rhyme with weather; but Burns's local patriotism for his native Kyle district of Ayrshire (or Coila as he apostrophises it poetically) combined with an eye for heather in his poem *To William Simpson, Ochiltree*, written in May 1785:

"We'll sing old Coila's plains and fells,
Her moors red-brown wi' heather bells,
Her banks an' braes, her dens an' dells,
Where glorious Wallace
Aft bure the gree, as story tells,
Frae Suthron billies."

It is interesting that Burns chooses to celebrate not the obvious purple splendour of the summer bloom of heather but the dun colour of the faded flower.

The Paisley poet Robert Tannahill, an admirer of Burns, also celebrated the Highlands and their heathery landscape in *The Braes o' Balquhither*:

"Let us go, lassie, go
To the braes o' Balquhither,
Where the blaeberries grow
'Mang the bonnie Highland heather;
Where the deer and the rae,
Lightly bounding together,
Sport the lang simmer day
On the braes o' Balquhither."

Alan Ramsay has a delightful reference to the national plant in his great pastoral poem of 1725, set in the Pentland Hills, *The Gentle Shepherd*:

d deer in heather

Golden eagle and pine marten

Although heather is widespread throughout Scotland, as may be seen in Border ballads such as *The Dowie Houms o' Yarrow*:

"Yestreen I dream'd a dolefu' dream;
I ken'd there wad be sorrow;
I dream'd I pu'd the heather green,
On the dowie banks o' Yarrow."

It is surely its associations with the mountains of the Highlands which have chiefly inspired our poets. For example, John Park's nostalgic celebration of the Aberdeenshire mountain of Bennachie, *Where Gadie Rins*:

"When corn grew yellow, and the hether-bells
Bloom'd bonny on the moor and rising fells,
Nae birns, or briers, or whins e'er troubled me,
Clif I cou'd find blae berries ripe for thee."

"I wish I were where Gadie rins,
'Mang fragrant heath and yellow whins,
Or, brawlin' doun the bosky linns,
At the back o' Benochie."

Even that loyal Borderer Walter Scott's invocation of *My Own, My Native Land* has the feel of the true heathery Highlands about it:

"O Caledonia! stern and wild,
Meet nurse for a poetic child!
Land of brown heath and shaggy wood,
Land of the mountain and the flood,
Land of my sires! what mortal hand
Can e'er untie the filial band
That knits me to thy rugged strand."

Such a poet of the hills as Robert Louis Stevenson could not, of course, fail to mention heather – although he does so less specifically and less often than one might imagine. The plant is mentioned in poems like *The Song of the Sword of Alan* from *Kidnapped*:

"Come to me from the hills of heather,
Come from the isles of the sea.
O far-beholding eagles,
Here is your meat".

It is, however, in heather's contribution to the overall idea of the hill country that Stevenson's most memorable lines come:

"O to mount again where erst I haunted;
Where the old red hills are bird-enchanted..." (*In the Highlands*)

and, perhaps in the poem that most poignantly expresses the exile's longing for the hills of home – a poem dedicated to the Scottish novelist-clergyman S.R. Crockett:

"Blows the wind today, and the sun and the rain are flying,
Blows the wind on the moors

today and now,
Where about the graves of
the martyrs the whaups are
crying,
My heart remembers how!

Grey recumbent tombs of the
dead in desert places,
Standing-stones of the
vacant wine-red moor,
Hills of sheep, and the howes
of the silent vanished races,
And winds, austere and pure:

Be it granted me to behold
you again in dying,
Hills of home! and to hear
again the call;
Hear about the graves of the
martyrs the peewees crying,
And hear no more at all."

As one might expect, poets in
the Gaelic tradition have
been noted for their
celebration of heather. Henry
Whyte translated *The Isle of
the Heather* from the Gaelic of
Murdo Macleaod:

"I wish I were now
In the isle of the sea,
The Isle of the Heather,
And happy I'd be.

With deer on its mountains,
And fish in its rills,
Where heroes haved lived
'Mong its heath-covered
hills."

Sheriff Alexander Nicolson,
a nineteenth-century lawyer
and Gaelic scholar (and
surely one of the few
Scottish poets to have a
mountain named after him –
Sgurr Alasdair, Alexander's
Peak, the highest summit in
the Cuillins of his native
Skye) wrote in *The Heather*:

"O sweet is the breath of the
heather
On the braes of the
highlands that blows;
O rich is its bloom when at
evening
The hills glow in purple and
rose.

ghlander above Loch Etive

I sit on the slopes of Loch
Etive,
The heather is up to my
knees;
I look to the West where the
islands
Arise from the far gloaming
sea.

Here, wrapped in my plaid
in the heather,
I envy no monarch his bed,
Come dream of the hills and
the Highlands,
And visit in slumber my
bed."

Another Scots writer, deeply
influenced by the Gaelic
tradition, whose thoughts
turned naturally to heather,
was the Argyll-born poet and
novelist Neil Munro, who
dedicated a whole poem
– The Heather – to the
subject:

"If I were King of France,
that noble fine land,
And the gold was elbow deep
within my chests,
And my castles lay in scores
along the wine-land
With towers as high where
the eagle nests;
If harpers sweet, and
swordsmen stout and
vaunting,
My history sang, my
stainless tartan wore,
Was not my fortune poor
with one thing wanting –
The heather at my door?

My galleys might be sailing
every ocean,
Robbing the isles, and
sacking hold and keep;
My chevaliers go prancing at
my notion
To bring me back of cattle,
horse and sheep;
Fond arms be round my
neck, the young heart's
tether,
And true love kisses all the
night might fill,
But oh! mochree, if I had not
the heather,

Before me on the hill!
A hunter's fate is all I would
be craving,
A shepherd's plaiding and a
beggar's pay,
If I might earn them where
the heather's waving,
Gives fragrance to the day.
The stars might see me,
homeless one and weary,
Without a roof to fend me
from the dew,
And still content, I'd find a
bedding cheery
Where'er the heather grew."

Of course it is not only
Scottish poets who have used
the heather in their verse.
On his brief visit in 1881 to
Loch Lomond, which
resulted in the marvellous
outpouring of *Inversnaid*,
Gerard Manley Hopkins had
an eye for the surroundings
of his burn and waterfall:

"Degged with dew, dappled
with dew
Are the groins of the braes

that the brook treads
through,
Wiry heathpacks, flitches of
fern
And the beadbonny ash that
sits over the burn."

In the twentieth century,
heather has continued to
feature in poetry and song
and it forms the point of
departure for Hugh
MacDiarmid's delightful and
thought-provoking
celebration of Scotland's
natural diversity, *Scotland
Small?*

"Scotland small? our
multiform, our infinite
Scotland small?
Only as a patch of hillside
may be a cliché corner
To a fool who cries 'Nothing
but heather!' where in
September another
Sitting there and resting and
gazing round
Sees not only the heather but

blaeberries
With bright green leaves and
leaves already turned scarlet,
Hiding ripe blue berries; and
amongst the sage-green
leaves
Of the bog-myrtle the golden
flowers of the tormentil
shining;
And on the small bare places,
where the little Blackface
sheep
Found grazing, milkworts
blue as summer skies;
And down in neglected peat-
hags, not worked
Within living memory,
sphagnum moss in pastel
shades
Of yellow, green, and pink;
sundew and butterwort
Waiting with wide-open
sticky leaves for their tiny
winged prey;
And nodding harebells vying
in their colour
With the blue butterflies that
poise themselves delicately
upon them,

And stunted rowans with
harsh dry leaves of glorious
colour.
'Nothing but heather!' –
How marvellously
descriptive! And
incomplete!"

The response to the heather,
extending from MacDiarmid
back some five and a half
centuries to William
Dunbar's:

"Grait abbais grayth I nill to
gather,
Bot ane kirk scant coverit
with hadder."

surely reflects the large part
that heather has played in
the everyday life of Scotland
and the place it has had in
the affections of those who,
like Henry Erskine, could
boast:

"In the garb of old Gaul,
wi' the fire of old Rome,
From the heath-cover'd of

mountains of Scotia we come,
Where the Romans
endeavour'd our country
to gain,
But our ancestors fought,
and they fought not in vain!"

ACKNOWLEDGMENT

Scotland Small? *by Hugh
MacDiarmid appears by permission
of his estate and is taken from his*
Collected Poems, *published
by Carcanet Press Ltd.*